50 Delicious Stew Dishes for Home

By: Kelly Johnson

Table of Contents

- Classic Beef Stew
- Chicken and Dumplings Stew
- Hearty Vegetable Stew
- Lamb Stew with Root Vegetables
- Irish Guinness Stew
- Hungarian Goulash
- French Coq au Vin
- Italian Osso Buco Stew
- Moroccan Lamb Tagine
- Spicy Cajun Gumbo
- Slow-Cooked Pork and Bean Stew
- Creamy Seafood Chowder
- Thai Green Curry Stew
- Korean Kimchi Jjigae
- Indian Chicken Curry Stew
- Jamaican Oxtail Stew
- Brazilian Feijoada
- Mexican Pozole Rojo
- Spanish Fabada Asturiana
- Japanese Nikujaga (Beef and Potato Stew)
- Ethiopian Doro Wat
- Russian Beef Stroganoff Stew
- Filipino Kare-Kare (Peanut Stew)
- Portuguese Caldo Verde
- Turkish Lamb and Chickpea Stew
- Lebanese Beef and Okra Stew
- Caribbean Callaloo Stew
- Peruvian Seco de Cordero
- Southern Brunswick Stew
- Greek Youvetsi (Beef and Orzo Stew)
- Egyptian Lentil and Tomato Stew
- Swedish Kalops (Beef and Spice Stew)
- Polish Bigos (Hunter's Stew)
- Vietnamese Bò Kho (Beef and Carrot Stew)
- Tunisian Chickpea and Harissa Stew

- Malaysian Laksa Stew
- Afghan Korma Stew
- Norwegian Fiskesuppe (Fish Stew)
- Georgian Chakhokhbili (Chicken Stew)
- Persian Fesenjan (Walnut and Pomegranate Stew)
- Basque Piperade Stew
- Ukrainian Borscht
- Belgian Carbonnade Flamande
- Indonesian Rendang
- Swiss Cheese and Onion Stew
- Cuban Ropa Vieja
- South African Bunny Chow Stew
- Middle Eastern Harira (Lentil and Lamb Stew)
- Scottish Cullen Skink (Smoked Fish Stew)
- Hawaiian Loco Moco Stew

Classic Beef Stew

Ingredients:

- 2 lbs beef chuck, cubed
- 3 tbsp flour
- 2 tbsp olive oil
- 1 onion, chopped
- 3 carrots, sliced
- 3 potatoes, cubed
- 2 cloves garlic, minced
- 4 cups beef broth
- 1 cup red wine
- 2 tbsp tomato paste
- 1 tsp thyme
- 1 bay leaf
- Salt & pepper to taste

Instructions:

1. Toss beef in flour, salt, and pepper.
2. Heat oil in a pot and brown beef. Remove and set aside.
3. Sauté onion, garlic, and tomato paste. Add wine and scrape the pan.
4. Return beef, add broth, thyme, bay leaf, carrots, and potatoes.
5. Simmer for 2 hours until tender.

Chicken and Dumplings Stew

Ingredients:

- 1 lb chicken thighs, diced
- 1 onion, chopped
- 3 carrots, sliced
- 2 celery stalks, chopped
- 4 cups chicken broth
- 1 cup milk
- 2 tbsp butter
- 1 cup flour
- 1 tsp baking powder
- 1/2 tsp salt
- 1/2 cup milk (for dumplings)
- 1 tbsp parsley

Instructions:

1. Sauté onion, carrots, and celery in butter.
2. Add chicken, broth, salt, and pepper. Simmer for 30 minutes.
3. Mix flour, baking powder, salt, and milk to make dumplings.
4. Drop spoonfuls into stew, cover, and cook for 15 minutes.

Hearty Vegetable Stew

Ingredients:

- 1 onion, chopped
- 2 carrots, sliced
- 2 potatoes, cubed
- 1 zucchini, sliced
- 1 can diced tomatoes
- 4 cups vegetable broth
- 2 cloves garlic, minced
- 1 tsp thyme
- 1 bay leaf
- Salt & pepper to taste

Instructions:

1. Sauté onion and garlic in olive oil.
2. Add carrots, potatoes, tomatoes, broth, and spices.
3. Simmer for 30 minutes.
4. Add zucchini and cook for 10 more minutes.

Lamb Stew with Root Vegetables

Ingredients:

- 2 lbs lamb, cubed
- 1 onion, chopped
- 3 carrots, sliced
- 2 parsnips, chopped
- 3 potatoes, cubed
- 4 cups beef broth
- 1 tbsp tomato paste
- 1 tsp rosemary
- 1 bay leaf
- Salt & pepper

Instructions:

1. Brown lamb in a pot. Remove and set aside.
2. Sauté onion and tomato paste. Add broth and spices.
3. Return lamb and simmer for 1 hour.
4. Add vegetables and cook for 30 more minutes.

Irish Guinness Stew

Ingredients:

- 2 lbs beef chuck, cubed
- 1 onion, chopped
- 3 carrots, sliced
- 3 potatoes, cubed
- 1 can Guinness beer
- 4 cups beef broth
- 2 tbsp tomato paste
- 1 tsp thyme
- Salt & pepper

Instructions:

1. Brown beef and remove.
2. Sauté onion and tomato paste. Add Guinness and deglaze.
3. Return beef and add broth, thyme, carrots, and potatoes.
4. Simmer for 2 hours.

Hungarian Goulash

Ingredients:

- 2 lbs beef chuck, cubed
- 2 onions, chopped
- 3 cloves garlic, minced
- 2 tbsp paprika
- 4 cups beef broth
- 1 can diced tomatoes
- 3 potatoes, cubed
- 2 carrots, sliced
- 1 tsp caraway seeds
- Salt & pepper

Instructions:

1. Brown beef and remove.
2. Sauté onions and garlic, then add paprika.
3. Return beef, add broth, tomatoes, and spices. Simmer for 1.5 hours.
4. Add potatoes and carrots, cook for 30 more minutes.

French Coq au Vin

Ingredients:

- 1 whole chicken, cut into pieces
- 1 onion, chopped
- 2 carrots, sliced
- 4 cloves garlic, minced
- 1 bottle red wine
- 2 cups chicken broth
- 2 tbsp tomato paste
- 1 bay leaf
- 1 tsp thyme
- Salt & pepper

Instructions:

1. Brown chicken pieces and remove.
2. Sauté onions, carrots, and garlic. Add tomato paste.
3. Return chicken, add wine, broth, and spices. Simmer for 1.5 hours.

Italian Osso Buco Stew

Ingredients:

- 2 veal shanks
- 1 onion, chopped
- 2 carrots, sliced
- 2 cloves garlic, minced
- 1 cup white wine
- 3 cups beef broth
- 1 can diced tomatoes
- 1 tsp rosemary
- 1 bay leaf
- Salt & pepper

Instructions:

1. Brown veal shanks and remove.
2. Sauté onion, garlic, and carrots. Add wine and deglaze.
3. Return veal, add broth, tomatoes, and spices. Simmer for 2 hours.

Moroccan Lamb Tagine

Ingredients:

- 2 lbs lamb, cubed
- 1 onion, chopped
- 3 cloves garlic, minced
- 2 carrots, sliced
- 1 can chickpeas
- 1 cup dried apricots
- 4 cups beef broth
- 1 tsp cinnamon
- 1 tsp cumin
- Salt & pepper

Instructions:

1. Brown lamb and remove.
2. Sauté onion, garlic, and carrots. Add spices.
3. Return lamb, add broth, chickpeas, and apricots. Simmer for 1.5 hours.

Spicy Cajun Gumbo

Ingredients:

- 1 lb andouille sausage, sliced
- 1 lb chicken, diced
- 1 onion, chopped
- 1 green bell pepper, chopped
- 2 stalks celery, chopped
- 4 cloves garlic, minced
- ¼ cup flour
- 4 cups chicken broth
- 1 can diced tomatoes
- 1 tsp cayenne pepper
- 1 bay leaf
- 1 tsp thyme
- 1 cup okra, sliced
- Salt & pepper

Instructions:

1. Brown sausage and chicken, remove.
2. Make a roux by stirring flour in oil until brown.
3. Add onion, bell pepper, celery, and garlic.
4. Return meat, add broth, tomatoes, and spices. Simmer for 1 hour.
5. Add okra and cook for 10 more minutes.

Slow-Cooked Pork and Bean Stew

Ingredients:

- 2 lbs pork shoulder, cubed
- 1 onion, chopped
- 3 cloves garlic, minced
- 2 cans white beans, drained
- 4 cups chicken broth
- 1 can diced tomatoes
- 1 tsp smoked paprika
- 1 tsp cumin
- 1 bay leaf
- Salt & pepper

Instructions:

1. Brown pork in a slow cooker on high.
2. Add onions, garlic, beans, broth, tomatoes, and spices.
3. Cook on low for 6-8 hours.

Creamy Seafood Chowder

Ingredients:

- 1 lb mixed seafood (shrimp, clams, cod)
- 1 onion, chopped
- 2 potatoes, diced
- 3 cups seafood broth
- 1 cup heavy cream
- 2 tbsp butter
- 1 tsp thyme
- Salt & pepper

Instructions:

1. Sauté onion in butter, then add potatoes and broth.
2. Simmer until potatoes are soft, then add seafood.
3. Stir in cream and season.

Thai Green Curry Stew

Ingredients:

- 1 lb chicken, sliced
- 1 onion, chopped
- 1 can coconut milk
- 2 tbsp green curry paste
- 1 cup chicken broth
- 1 bell pepper, sliced
- 1 zucchini, sliced
- 1 tbsp fish sauce
- 1 tbsp lime juice
- Fresh basil

Instructions:

1. Sauté onion and curry paste.
2. Add chicken, broth, and coconut milk.
3. Simmer for 15 minutes, then add vegetables.
4. Finish with fish sauce, lime juice, and basil.

Korean Kimchi Jjigae

Ingredients:

- 1 cup kimchi, chopped
- 1/2 lb pork belly, sliced
- 1 onion, chopped
- 3 cups water
- 1 tbsp gochujang (Korean chili paste)
- 1 tbsp soy sauce
- 1 tsp sugar
- 1 block tofu, cubed
- Green onions

Instructions:

1. Sauté pork, onion, and kimchi.
2. Add water, gochujang, soy sauce, and sugar.
3. Simmer for 20 minutes, then add tofu and green onions.

Indian Chicken Curry Stew

Ingredients:

- 1 lb chicken, cubed
- 1 onion, chopped
- 2 cloves garlic, minced
- 1 can diced tomatoes
- 1 cup coconut milk
- 1 tbsp curry powder
- 1 tsp turmeric
- 1 tsp cumin
- 1 cup chicken broth

Instructions:

1. Sauté onion and garlic.
2. Add chicken, curry powder, turmeric, and cumin.
3. Pour in tomatoes, broth, and coconut milk. Simmer for 30 minutes.

Jamaican Oxtail Stew

Ingredients:

- 2 lbs oxtail, cut into pieces
- 1 onion, chopped
- 2 cloves garlic, minced
- 1 can kidney beans
- 4 cups beef broth
- 1 tbsp allspice
- 1 scotch bonnet pepper, whole
- 1 tsp thyme
- 1 carrot, sliced

Instructions:

1. Brown oxtail and remove.
2. Sauté onion and garlic.
3. Return oxtail, add broth, beans, spices, and carrot.
4. Simmer for 3 hours.

Brazilian Feijoada

Ingredients:

- 1 lb black beans, soaked
- 1 lb pork shoulder, cubed
- 1/2 lb smoked sausage, sliced
- 1 onion, chopped
- 3 cloves garlic, minced
- 4 cups beef broth
- 1 bay leaf
- 1 tsp cumin
- Salt & pepper

Instructions:

1. Sauté onion and garlic.
2. Add pork, sausage, and beans.
3. Pour in broth, add bay leaf and cumin.
4. Simmer for 2 hours.

Mexican Pozole Rojo

Ingredients:

- 2 lbs pork shoulder, cubed
- 1 onion, chopped
- 3 cloves garlic, minced
- 1 can hominy
- 4 cups chicken broth
- 2 dried guajillo chilies, blended
- 1 tsp oregano
- 1 tsp cumin
- Radishes and cabbage for garnish

Instructions:

1. Brown pork, then add onion and garlic.
2. Pour in broth, hominy, and chili paste.
3. Simmer for 2 hours and garnish with radishes and cabbage.

Spanish Fabada Asturiana

Ingredients:

- 1 lb white beans, soaked
- 1/2 lb chorizo, sliced
- 1/2 lb pork belly, cubed
- 1 onion, chopped
- 3 cloves garlic, minced
- 4 cups chicken broth
- 1 bay leaf
- Salt & pepper

Instructions:

1. Sauté chorizo and pork belly.
2. Add onion, garlic, and beans.
3. Pour in broth and add bay leaf. Simmer for 2 hours.

Japanese Nikujaga (Beef and Potato Stew)

Ingredients:

- 1/2 lb beef, thinly sliced
- 2 potatoes, cubed
- 1 onion, sliced
- 2 cups dashi broth
- 2 tbsp soy sauce
- 1 tbsp mirin
- 1 tbsp sugar
- 1 carrot, sliced

Instructions:

1. Sauté beef and onion.
2. Add potatoes, carrots, and broth.
3. Pour in soy sauce, mirin, and sugar. Simmer for 30 minutes.

Ethiopian Doro Wat

Ingredients:

- 2 lbs chicken, cut into pieces
- 2 onions, finely chopped
- 3 tbsp berbere spice
- 3 tbsp niter kibbeh (Ethiopian spiced butter)
- 3 cloves garlic, minced
- 1 tbsp ginger, minced
- 1 cup chicken broth
- 4 hard-boiled eggs
- Salt to taste

Instructions:

1. Sauté onions in a dry pan until soft.
2. Add niter kibbeh, garlic, and ginger.
3. Stir in berbere spice and chicken.
4. Pour in broth and simmer for 40 minutes.
5. Add eggs and cook for 10 more minutes.

Russian Beef Stroganoff Stew

Ingredients:

- 1.5 lbs beef sirloin, sliced thinly
- 1 onion, chopped
- 2 cloves garlic, minced
- 1 cup beef broth
- 1 cup sour cream
- 1 tbsp mustard
- 1/2 cup mushrooms, sliced
- 1 tbsp butter
- Salt & pepper

Instructions:

1. Brown beef in butter and remove.
2. Sauté onions, garlic, and mushrooms.
3. Add beef broth, mustard, and sour cream.
4. Return beef and simmer for 15 minutes.

Filipino Kare-Kare (Peanut Stew)

Ingredients:

- 1 lb oxtail (or beef shank)
- 1 onion, chopped
- 2 cloves garlic, minced
- 1 cup peanut butter
- 4 cups beef broth
- 1 tbsp annatto powder
- 1 cup eggplant, sliced
- 1/2 cup green beans
- 1/2 cup bok choy
- 1 tbsp fish sauce

Instructions:

1. Boil oxtail in broth for 2 hours.
2. Sauté onion, garlic, and annatto powder.
3. Stir in peanut butter, then add oxtail and broth.
4. Add vegetables and cook until tender.

Portuguese Caldo Verde

Ingredients:

- 1 lb potatoes, diced
- 1 onion, chopped
- 2 cloves garlic, minced
- 4 cups chicken broth
- 1/2 lb chorizo, sliced
- 2 cups kale, chopped
- 1 tbsp olive oil
- Salt & pepper

Instructions:

1. Sauté onions and garlic.
2. Add potatoes and broth. Simmer until soft.
3. Blend until smooth.
4. Stir in chorizo and kale. Cook for 10 minutes.

Turkish Lamb and Chickpea Stew

Ingredients:

- 1 lb lamb, cubed
- 1 onion, chopped
- 2 cloves garlic, minced
- 1 can chickpeas, drained
- 2 cups beef broth
- 1 can diced tomatoes
- 1 tsp cumin
- 1 tsp paprika
- Salt & pepper

Instructions:

1. Brown lamb and remove.
2. Sauté onion and garlic.
3. Add lamb, chickpeas, broth, tomatoes, and spices.
4. Simmer for 1 hour.

Lebanese Beef and Okra Stew

Ingredients:

- 1 lb beef, cubed
- 1 onion, chopped
- 2 cloves garlic, minced
- 1 can diced tomatoes
- 2 cups beef broth
- 1 cup okra, trimmed
- 1 tsp allspice
- 1/2 tsp cinnamon
- Salt & pepper

Instructions:

1. Brown beef and remove.
2. Sauté onions and garlic.
3. Add beef, tomatoes, broth, and spices.
4. Simmer for 1 hour, then add okra. Cook for 15 minutes.

Caribbean Callaloo Stew

Ingredients:

- 1 bunch callaloo (or spinach), chopped
- 1 onion, chopped
- 2 cloves garlic, minced
- 1 can coconut milk
- 1 cup chicken broth
- 1 scotch bonnet pepper, whole
- 1 tbsp thyme
- 1/2 cup okra, sliced
- Salt & pepper

Instructions:

1. Sauté onion and garlic.
2. Add callaloo, coconut milk, broth, and pepper.
3. Simmer for 20 minutes, then add okra.

Peruvian Seco de Cordero

Ingredients:

- 1.5 lbs lamb shoulder, cubed
- 1 onion, chopped
- 2 cloves garlic, minced
- 1 cup cilantro, blended with 1/2 cup water
- 2 cups beef broth
- 1/2 cup beer
- 1 tsp cumin
- 1 tsp paprika
- 1 cup peas
- 1 carrot, sliced

Instructions:

1. Brown lamb and remove.
2. Sauté onion, garlic, and spices.
3. Add cilantro blend, broth, and beer.
4. Return lamb, simmer for 1 hour.
5. Add peas and carrots, cook 10 minutes.

Southern Brunswick Stew

Ingredients:

- 1 lb shredded chicken
- 1/2 lb pulled pork
- 1 onion, chopped
- 2 cloves garlic, minced
- 1 can diced tomatoes
- 1 cup corn
- 1 cup lima beans
- 2 cups chicken broth
- 1 tbsp Worcestershire sauce
- 1 tbsp hot sauce

Instructions:

1. Sauté onions and garlic.
2. Add chicken, pork, tomatoes, and broth.
3. Stir in Worcestershire and hot sauce.
4. Simmer for 30 minutes, add vegetables.

Greek Youvetsi (Beef and Orzo Stew)

Ingredients:

- 1.5 lbs beef, cubed
- 1 onion, chopped
- 2 cloves garlic, minced
- 1 can diced tomatoes
- 2 cups beef broth
- 1 cup orzo pasta
- 1 tsp cinnamon
- 1 tsp oregano
- Grated kefalotyri cheese

Instructions:

1. Brown beef and remove.
2. Sauté onion and garlic.
3. Add beef, tomatoes, broth, and spices. Simmer 1 hour.
4. Stir in orzo and cook for 15 minutes.
5. Top with cheese before serving.

Egyptian Lentil and Tomato Stew

Ingredients:

- 1 cup red lentils
- 1 onion, chopped
- 2 cloves garlic, minced
- 1 can diced tomatoes
- 4 cups vegetable broth
- 1 tsp cumin
- 1/2 tsp cinnamon
- 1/2 tsp paprika
- 1 tbsp olive oil
- Salt & pepper

Instructions:

1. Sauté onion and garlic in olive oil.
2. Add lentils, tomatoes, broth, and spices.
3. Simmer for 25-30 minutes, stirring occasionally.

Swedish Kalops (Beef and Spice Stew)

Ingredients:

- 1.5 lbs beef, cubed
- 1 onion, chopped
- 2 cloves garlic, minced
- 2 cups beef broth
- 1 carrot, sliced
- 5 whole allspice berries
- 2 bay leaves
- 1 tbsp butter
- Salt & pepper

Instructions:

1. Brown beef in butter.
2. Sauté onions and garlic.
3. Add broth, spices, and carrots.
4. Simmer for 1.5 hours until tender.

Polish Bigos (Hunter's Stew)

Ingredients:

- 1 lb pork shoulder, cubed
- 1/2 lb kielbasa, sliced
- 1 onion, chopped
- 2 cups sauerkraut, drained
- 1 can diced tomatoes
- 1 cup beef broth
- 1 tsp caraway seeds
- 1/2 tsp paprika
- 1 tbsp butter

Instructions:

1. Brown pork and kielbasa in butter.
2. Sauté onions, then add sauerkraut and tomatoes.
3. Stir in broth and spices. Simmer for 1.5 hours.

Vietnamese Bò Kho (Beef and Carrot Stew)

Ingredients:

- 1.5 lbs beef, cubed
- 1 onion, chopped
- 2 cloves garlic, minced
- 2 cups beef broth
- 1 tbsp fish sauce
- 1 tbsp tomato paste
- 2 carrots, sliced
- 1 cinnamon stick
- 2 star anise
- 1 tbsp lemongrass, minced

Instructions:

1. Brown beef and remove.
2. Sauté onion, garlic, and lemongrass.
3. Add beef, broth, tomato paste, and spices.
4. Simmer for 1.5 hours, then add carrots.

Tunisian Chickpea and Harissa Stew

Ingredients:

- 1 can chickpeas, drained
- 1 onion, chopped
- 2 cloves garlic, minced
- 1 can diced tomatoes
- 2 cups vegetable broth
- 1 tbsp harissa paste
- 1 tsp cumin
- 1/2 tsp coriander
- 1 tbsp olive oil

Instructions:

1. Sauté onion and garlic in olive oil.
2. Stir in harissa, tomatoes, and broth.
3. Add chickpeas and spices. Simmer for 25 minutes.

Malaysian Laksa Stew

Ingredients:

- 1 lb shrimp or chicken
- 1 onion, chopped
- 2 cloves garlic, minced
- 2 tbsp laksa paste
- 4 cups coconut milk
- 2 cups chicken broth
- 1/2 cup bean sprouts
- 1 tbsp fish sauce
- 1 lime, juiced

Instructions:

1. Sauté onion and garlic.
2. Stir in laksa paste, coconut milk, and broth.
3. Add protein, fish sauce, and simmer for 20 minutes.
4. Serve with bean sprouts and lime.

Afghan Korma Stew

Ingredients:

- 1 lb lamb, cubed
- 1 onion, chopped
- 2 cloves garlic, minced
- 1 can diced tomatoes
- 2 cups beef broth
- 1 tsp turmeric
- 1 tsp cumin
- 1/2 tsp cardamom
- 1 tbsp ghee

Instructions:

1. Brown lamb in ghee.
2. Sauté onions and garlic.
3. Add tomatoes, broth, and spices.
4. Simmer for 1.5 hours until tender.

Norwegian Fiskesuppe (Fish Stew)

Ingredients:

- 1 lb white fish, cubed
- 1 onion, chopped
- 2 cups fish stock
- 1 cup heavy cream
- 1 carrot, sliced
- 1 potato, diced
- 1 tbsp butter
- 1 tbsp dill, chopped
- Salt & pepper

Instructions:

1. Sauté onion in butter.
2. Add fish stock, potato, and carrot. Simmer for 10 minutes.
3. Stir in cream, fish, and dill. Cook until fish is tender.

Georgian Chakhokhbili (Chicken Stew)

Ingredients:

- 1.5 lbs chicken, cut into pieces
- 1 onion, chopped
- 2 cloves garlic, minced
- 1 can diced tomatoes
- 1 cup chicken broth
- 1 tsp coriander
- 1 tsp paprika
- 1/2 cup fresh cilantro, chopped
- Salt & pepper

Instructions:

1. Brown chicken and remove.
2. Sauté onions and garlic.
3. Add tomatoes, broth, and spices.
4. Return chicken and simmer for 40 minutes.
5. Garnish with cilantro.

Persian Fesenjan (Walnut and Pomegranate Stew)

Ingredients:

- 1 lb chicken, cut into pieces
- 1 onion, chopped
- 2 cloves garlic, minced
- 1 cup ground walnuts
- 1 cup pomegranate molasses
- 2 cups chicken broth
- 1/2 tsp cinnamon
- 1/2 tsp turmeric
- 1 tbsp olive oil

Instructions:

1. Brown chicken in olive oil.
2. Sauté onions and garlic.
3. Add walnuts, broth, and pomegranate molasses.
4. Return chicken and simmer for 45 minutes.

Basque Piperade Stew

Ingredients:

- 1 onion, chopped
- 2 bell peppers, sliced
- 2 cloves garlic, minced
- 1 can diced tomatoes
- 1 tbsp olive oil
- 1 tsp paprika
- 1/2 tsp thyme
- Salt & pepper

Instructions:

1. Sauté onions, garlic, and peppers in olive oil.
2. Add tomatoes, spices, and simmer for 20 minutes.

Ukrainian Borscht

Ingredients:

- 3 medium beets, shredded
- 1 onion, chopped
- 2 cloves garlic, minced
- 1 large carrot, shredded
- 2 potatoes, diced
- 1/2 small cabbage, shredded
- 1 can diced tomatoes
- 4 cups beef or vegetable broth
- 1 tbsp vinegar
- 1 tbsp sugar
- 2 tbsp olive oil
- Salt & pepper
- Sour cream & fresh dill for garnish

Instructions:

1. Sauté onion, garlic, and carrot in olive oil.
2. Add broth, beets, potatoes, cabbage, and tomatoes.
3. Stir in vinegar, sugar, salt, and pepper. Simmer for 45 minutes.
4. Serve with sour cream and fresh dill.

Belgian Carbonnade Flamande

Ingredients:

- 2 lbs beef chuck, cubed
- 2 onions, sliced
- 2 cups beef broth
- 1 bottle dark beer
- 2 tbsp Dijon mustard
- 2 tbsp brown sugar
- 2 tbsp butter
- 2 bay leaves
- 1 tbsp thyme
- Salt & pepper

Instructions:

1. Brown beef in butter. Remove and sauté onions.
2. Return beef, add beer, broth, mustard, sugar, and spices.
3. Simmer for 2 hours until tender.

Indonesian Rendang

Ingredients:

- 2 lbs beef, cubed
- 1 onion, chopped
- 3 cloves garlic, minced
- 1 can coconut milk
- 2 tbsp rendang spice paste
- 1 tbsp ginger, minced
- 1 tsp turmeric
- 2 kaffir lime leaves
- 1 cinnamon stick

Instructions:

1. Sauté onion, garlic, and ginger.
2. Add beef, coconut milk, spices, and lime leaves.
3. Simmer for 2 hours until thickened.

Swiss Cheese and Onion Stew

Ingredients:

- 2 onions, sliced
- 2 cloves garlic, minced
- 2 cups beef or vegetable broth
- 1 cup white wine
- 1 cup heavy cream
- 1 ½ cups Swiss cheese, grated
- 1 tbsp butter
- Salt & pepper
- Croutons for serving

Instructions:

1. Sauté onions and garlic in butter.
2. Add broth, wine, and simmer for 20 minutes.
3. Stir in cream and cheese until melted.
4. Serve with croutons.

Cuban Ropa Vieja

Ingredients:

- 2 lbs flank steak
- 1 onion, sliced
- 2 cloves garlic, minced
- 1 bell pepper, sliced
- 1 can diced tomatoes
- 1 cup beef broth
- 1 tbsp cumin
- 1 tsp smoked paprika
- 1 tbsp vinegar
- 1 tbsp olive oil

Instructions:

1. Brown steak in oil, remove, and shred.
2. Sauté onion, garlic, and bell pepper.
3. Add tomatoes, broth, spices, and return beef.
4. Simmer for 1.5 hours.

South African Bunny Chow Stew

Ingredients:

- 1 lb chicken or lamb, cubed
- 1 onion, chopped
- 2 cloves garlic, minced
- 2 tbsp curry powder
- 1 can diced tomatoes
- 1 cup chicken broth
- 1 potato, diced
- 1 tbsp vegetable oil
- 1 loaf bread, hollowed out

Instructions:

1. Sauté onion and garlic in oil.
2. Add meat, curry powder, tomatoes, broth, and potatoes.
3. Simmer for 45 minutes.
4. Serve inside the hollowed-out bread.

Middle Eastern Harira (Lentil and Lamb Stew)

Ingredients:

- 1 lb lamb, cubed
- 1 onion, chopped
- 2 cloves garlic, minced
- 1 can diced tomatoes
- 1 cup lentils
- 4 cups broth
- 1 tsp cumin
- 1 tsp cinnamon
- 1 tbsp olive oil

Instructions:

1. Brown lamb, remove.
2. Sauté onion, garlic, and spices.
3. Add tomatoes, broth, and lentils.
4. Return lamb and simmer for 1 hour.

Scottish Cullen Skink (Smoked Fish Stew)

Ingredients:

- 1 lb smoked haddock, flaked
- 1 onion, chopped
- 2 cups fish broth
- 1 cup milk
- 1 potato, diced
- 1 tbsp butter
- 1/2 cup heavy cream
- Salt & pepper
- Chives for garnish

Instructions:

1. Sauté onion in butter.
2. Add broth, milk, and potato. Simmer for 15 minutes.
3. Stir in haddock and cream. Heat through.
4. Garnish with chives.

Hawaiian Loco Moco Stew

Ingredients:

- 1 lb ground beef
- 1 onion, chopped
- 2 cloves garlic, minced
- 2 cups beef broth
- 1 tbsp Worcestershire sauce
- 2 tbsp soy sauce
- 1 tbsp butter

- 2 tbsp flour
- 4 fried eggs (for serving)
- Cooked rice (for serving)

Instructions:

1. Brown beef and remove.
2. Sauté onion and garlic in butter.
3. Stir in flour, then add broth, Worcestershire, and soy sauce.
4. Return beef, simmer for 20 minutes.
5. Serve over rice with a fried egg on top.

www.ingramcontent.com/pod-product-compliance
Lightning Source LLC
LaVergne TN
LVHW081336060526
838201LV00055B/2671